seventeen

college goals

AN INSIDER'S GUIDE TO FINDING AND GETTING INTO A SCHOOL YOU'LL LOVE

Bluestreak BOOKS

Bluestreak Books is an imprint of Weldon Owen,
a Bonnier Publishing USA company
www.bonnierpublishingusa.com

Edited and designed by Girl Friday Productions
www.girlfridayproductions.com

Library of Congress Cataloging in Publication data is available.

ISBN-13: 978-1-68188-407-3

First Printed in 2018
10 9 8 7 6 5 4 3 2 1
2018 2019 2020 2021

Printed in China

introduction

The only thing standing between you and that college life is figuring out where you might want to go, completing your applications, writing a killer essay, scoring solid test scores, shining in your activities, getting glowing recommendations, and . . . okay, that's a lot. But even though the process of getting accepted into college can seem big and overwhelming, it doesn't have to be.

That's where *Seventeen*'s *College Goals* comes in. This stress-free guide—part planner, part journal—will help walk you through the steps of applying to colleges. There are pages filled with practical cheat sheets, handy life hacks, thoughtful tips, fun quizzes, inspiring quotes from amazing women (including some of your favorite celebs), and prompts that will push you to self-reflect. (After all, that's what college essays are all about!) This way, you can freak out less about whether you'll get in, and actually start thinking about which school's offer you're going to accept.

junior year

JUNIOR YEAR
To-Do List

[ ] **Read a ton**—it helps with your vocab.

[ ] Take the **PSAT/NMSQT** in October.

[ ] Look into **SAT registration dates**, and plan on taking it in the spring.

[ ] **Speak up in class** so that your teachers know who you are. Then, at the end of the school year, ask two of your faves for letters of recommendation.

[ ] **Schedule meetings with your guidance counselor.** Give her a list of your activities and interests and ask her to suggest colleges for you.

[ ] Instead of throwing yourself into every activity at school, **choose what you've liked best so far and find a way to stand out**. If you're in the school band, you could organize a performance at a senior center. Or you could create a group, like a coding club or a body-positivity club, based on one of your passions.

[ ] **Start exploring colleges** online and going on visits.

[ ] **If there are subjects you love** (or if you have a dream career), then research schools that offer the best programs for those. But make sure they offer other areas of study, too, in case you change your mind.

[ ] If you haven't already, **sign up for challenging classes**—but don't overextend yourself. It's more important to do well in one AP subject than barely pass a handful of honors courses.

[ ] In March or April, **register for SAT Subject Tests and/or AP tests** in courses you've aced.

[ ] Talk to your parents about how you'll pay for college and **figure out your tuition budget**.

[ ] **Start looking into scholarships** (check out Chegg.com) and searching hashtags—#scholarshipchat, #scholarshipsearch, #scholarships—for other opportunities.

I CAN'T WAIT FOR...

1.

2.

3.

"When I am asked what I wish I had known as a teen, I always answer, 'STUDY, LEARN, EXPLORE. and find FRIENDS who want to study, learn, and explore with you.'"

—Sheryl Sandberg,
chief operating officer of Facebook

★ MY PERSONAL MOTTO ★
★ FOR JUNIOR YEAR: ★

DRINK MORE WATER

If you want to thrive in the year ahead—and all the ones after that—you've got to up your self-care game. Healthy habits are what make good times, good vibes, and good grades possible.

BE SELFISH WITH YOUR SLEEP

It's hard to be healthy and happy when you're not getting enough rest. You need to get eight to ten hours of shut-eye a night if you want to avoid the *tiredirritableunfocused* feels.

Make it happen: At night, first tackle the homework that requires you to be on the computer. (Blue light from screens messes up your ability to fall asleep.) Give yourself a screen-free hour before bedtime. Another snooze-worthy tip: Wash your face, brush your teeth, and do whatever is part of your bedtime routine way before you're ready to go to sleep. That way, when you're tired, you can just shut off the lights.

EAT REGULARLY—AND WELL

Skipping meals can mess with your ability to concentrate and your attitude—as your blood sugar plummets, so can your mood. Even worse, if you wait too long to eat, you're more likely to reach for processed, sugary foods that leave you cranky and zoned out.

Make it happen: Schedule school lunch dates with your bestie so you're less likely to ditch the caf. And for those days when you need to squeeze in extra study time, make sure you have a snack on hand. At home, keep a bowl of healthy treats in your kitchen so you can just grab one without thinking.

TAKE FIVE

Always being busy can mess with your mental health because it makes you feel out of control. (Hi, stress!) You may think it sounds woo woo or unimportant, but taking even just a few minutes for yourself can have big benefits.

Make it happen: Have a tried-and-true routine you can squeeze into your hectic schedule, even when you only have five minutes. Learn a few yoga moves you can do anywhere, such as lying on your back with your legs up the wall.

MOVE YOUR BODY

If you had to guess, how many hours a day do you spend sitting? Technology has, ironically, slowed us down, so you need to move to balance things out and keep your body happy.

Make it happen: You don't have to be captain of the cross-country team or the gymnastics MVP to get your heart pumping. Walk your dog around the block, go for a bike ride, take a boxing class—anything to get your blood pumping.

> ## "Sometimes you have to remind yourself to slow down and take care of yourself—breathe, and take a walk for five minutes."
>
> —Camila Cabello

_____
_____
_____
_____
_____
_____
_____
_____
_____
_____
_____
_____
_____
_____
_____
_____
_____
_____

9

QUIZ

How well do you take care of yourself?

1. **How many nights a week do you stay up late?**

   a. None—because beauty sleep!

   b. Not often, but hey, sometimes keeping up with your Snapstreaks can cause you to lose track of time.

   c. Almost. Every. Night. It's the only time you have to study.

2. **Have you ever skipped a meal because you were insanely busy?**

   a. Never. This girl gets hangry.

   b. You've been known to swap the salad bar for a study sesh from time to time.

   c. Yes, every day—the caf food totally sucks anyway.

3. **You're stressing over a paper that's due next week. Your plan:**

   a. Go for a run to clear your mind.

   b. Worry sick about it but still make time for a quick Netflix break.

   c. Huddle up in your room until it's done and you're sure it's A-worthy.

YOUR SCORE

Mostly As: You prioritize self-care, which is really great—it's key to feeling amazing.

Mostly Bs (or a mix of letters): You juggle a lot and can usually handle it, but sometimes your health takes a hit.

Mostly Cs: Girl, it's time to focus on *you*.

What are your TOP THREE favorite things to do for SELF-CARE?

1

....

....

This helps me: _____

_____

_____

_____

_____

_____

_____

_____

_____

_____

2 ....

This helps me: _____

_____

_____

_____

_____

_____

_____

_____

_____

_____

_____

3 ....

This helps me: _____

_____

_____

_____

_____

_____

_____

_____

_____

_____

What is ONE THING you could do to improve your self-care habits?

1 ....

....

How do you think this will help you? _____

_____

_____

_____

_____

_____

_____

_____

Have a two-pronged philosophy for self-care. 1. Do it because it makes you feel good. 2. Do it because being healthy will allow you to be more effective in every part of your life.

who are my favorites?
who knows me best?

Getting a Real Rec: Part 1

FAVE SUBJECTS THIS YEAR?

The only way to get recommendations that are meaningful and personal is to spend time with the teachers who might write them.

Introduce yourself.

If you haven't already gotten to know a couple of teachers you like, it's time to start. Pick at least one who teaches a subject you love and stop by their desk after class or send them an email with a thoughtful question. That way, you'll stand out, and later they'll be able to speak to your passions. For example, if you think you might want to study medicine, get to know your science teacher. They'll be able to talk about your enthusiasm and talent in biology or chemistry. Some schools require additional recommendations from peers, religious leaders, employers, coaches, or community members, so seek out people who know you well and can talk about how amazing you are.

Make your case.

Don't wait too long to ask—the more popular teachers are, the more likely it is they'll get lots of rec requests! Tell them about the schools you are considering, and let them know why their recommendation in particular would be meaningful to you.

CHEAT SHEET

important

Imagine you are a teacher writing a recommendation for *you*. What would you say? What are some positive things about you—personally, socially, and academically? Where do you see potential?

Write a draft here: _____

GET IT, GIRL

_____

_____

_____

_____

_____

_____

_____

_____

"As long as you look yourself in the mirror and know that you can make anything happen, you're good to go."

—Shay Mitchell

_____

_____

_____

_____

_____

_____

_____

_____

_____

Test Time

It's never too early to prep. As you know, there are two main types of standardized tests: **SAT** and **ACT**. Both measure what you learned in high school and are meant to show whether you are equipped to succeed in college.

The SAT

Do a practice test.

(a.k.a. the Scholastic Assessment Test)

The SAT has two sections: math and writing/language, plus an optional essay (some schools require it, some schools don't). This three-hour test (or three-hour, fifty-minutes, if you do the essay) has a max score of 1600—800 for math and 800 for reading. If you choose to do the essay, the score is based on three criteria (reading, writing, and analysis), worth an additional 8 points each.

For more information, visit collegereadiness.collegeboard.org/sat.

The ACT

STUDY TIME

(a.k.a. the American College Testing program)

A set of four multiple-choice tests (or five, if you take the optional writing test) that covers English, math, reading, *and* science, so if that's an area you love, it may be an opportunity to shine—and pump up your results. This is a three-hour test (or three-hour, forty-minutes, if you take the optional writing test), and the scoring is a little more complicated: Each section is scored between 1 and 36, and then averaged to generate a composite score. When it comes to the writing test, many feel the essay prompts are more straightforward than the SAT ones.

For more information, visit act.org.

*** Look up test prep courses/workshops.

Did we say just *two*?

To really show your stuff, consider taking the **SAT Subjects** and **AP** or **IB** tests.

SAT Subject Tests

Some schools require applicants to also take these. Each of the multiple-choice tests—there are 19 available—is one hour long. They fall under five general areas: English, history, languages, math, and science. Acing them can help you get noticed.

For more information, visit collegereadiness.collegeboard.org/sat-subject-tests.

AP (Advanced Placement) or IB (International Baccalaureate) Tests

Unlike the more general SAT and ACT, AP and IB tests are designed to show the knowledge you acquired during specific courses. AP tests are offered in 38 subjects. Most colleges don't require that you take these or report scores if you do, but if you do well (AP score of 3 or above, IB score of 4 or above), submitting them will not only help you get in, it might also get you advanced standing or college credit.

For more information, visit apstudent.collegeboard.org/home or ibo.org.

Testing Location & Dates:

You can find lots of great advice on how to study for and take tests. But when it comes down to it, everyone handles them differently. What are three test-taking strategies you've used with success in the past?

1 ....

This helps me: _____

_____

_____

_____

_____

Pay attention to your **POSTURE**! Sitting up straight will help boost your **CONCENTRATION**.

_____

_____

_____

_____

2 ....

This helps me: _____

_____

_____

_____

_____

_____

3 ....

This helps me: _____

_____

_____

_____

_____

_____

_____

_____

_____

_____

_____

_____

_____

_____

_____

_____

_____

LIFE HACK: BE STUDY SAVVY

Whether it's a few days or a few hours before a test, you can still pull off an epic study sesh!

PUT AWAY THE LAPTOP

When you use pen and paper to take notes, you're more likely to rephrase things in your own words and to focus on the important points. Writing takes longer and requires concentration, and it helps the info stick in your long-term memory.

GET PLENTY OF REST

Get eight to ten hours of sleep every night. Doing so will improve your concentration and ability to process new information, and help you retain what you learned.

BUST OUT YOUR HIGHLIGHTER

Review your notes and highlight the most important things. The visual element reinforces the information, and later you can quickly scan the crucial points.

GIVE IT A BREAK

Don't stay glued to your books. Learning in 1-hour blocks is most effective—50 minutes of studying followed by a 10-minute break. Every three hours, give your brain a breather—exercise, watch a show, or take a nap.

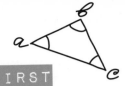

DO THE HARD STUFF FIRST

The longer you study, the more zoned out you'll get. So whatever you're struggling with the most—equations, biology terms, Spanish vocab—start there. That way you'll be focused and fresh when you need it the most.

TRY CHUNKING

It's not as gross as it sounds. Chunking is a study method that reduces information into broad categories. For example, see if you can memorize this sequence of numbers: 5556790213. Tough, right? Now try grouping: 555.679.0213. See? Easier! Do this with concepts, events, vocab words—anything you can divide into smaller chunks.

START FROM THE BOTTOM

When you always start studying from the beginning, you may never get to the stuff at the end. To make sure you cover everything, switch it up and start studying backward to forward. Now that's a genius move! Z, X, Y . . .

TALK ABOUT IT

Go over the info with a friend. Trying to explain concepts can reveal what you've retained and what you need to review again.

WHAT'S ON YOUR MIND?

QUIZ

Super-driven or just getting by: Which one are you?

1. **Do you live for your daily extracurricular?**

a. Totally! You wouldn't miss it for the world.

b. It's okay, but sometimes you don't feel like you're very good at it.

c. What afterschool activity?

2. **When was the last time you set a goal?**

a. Today! #Goals are your thing.

b. You've thought about it, but haven't actually done it yet.

c. Yeah, you're too busy for those.

3. **What's your aim when studying?**

a. To be able to explain stuff better than the teacher.

b. Learn enough to pass.

c. Cram it all in—and then keep your fingers crossed!

YOUR SCORE

Mostly As: Keep it up! Being good at something increases your confidence, which sets you up to feel amazing.

Mostly Bs (or a mix of letters): It might be time to challenge yourself in a new way.

Mostly Cs: Doing just enough won't make you feel very stellar. To learn how to be the boss you are, read on.

#GOALS

LIFE HACK: FIND YOUR PURPOSE

Having a sense of purpose can help you experience *real* bliss. This is how to find yours.

DO WHAT YOU GENUINELY LOVE

Juggling five activities because it looks good on applications or gets you lots of Insta-likes isn't genuine. Dedicate your time to something that matters to you. If it impresses a college, that's just a bonus.

HAVE A GOAL

Keep it realistic so you don't set yourself up for failure. The trick: Break a big goal into mini goals. For example, if you want to run a marathon, start by signing up for a 5K.

LOOK BEYOND THE PRAISE

Getting cred is not the only reason to do something. There's a difference between acing a test because you truly learned something and just doing it for the bragging rights.

GIVE YOURSELF KUDOS—ALWAYS

Hitting a goal you've worked hard for feels fantastic! So don't be shy about celebrating your wins. But find value in your losses too. No one can nail it every time—the key is to keep trying.

Building Your Résumé

You're way more than just a piece of paper—but a résumé still says a lot about you. It provides other people a quick and easy-to-read summary of what you're interested in and how you spend your time, and it's a good way for you to keep track of your accomplishments.

Before putting together your résumé, use this space to brainstorm some of the things you'd like to include. It can be anything, both in school and out—babysitting, starting your own band, competing for the debate team. Note your role and for how long you participated. For example:

Girl Up: member, 10th grade–present; 2–4 hours/week

As Social Media Chair, maintained and updated content on Facebook, Instagram, Twitter, and Snapchat for Girl Up club. Publicized events (i.e., fundraisers, advocacy boot camps, and meetings) on social media and by email. Attended weekly executive board meetings with club leaders. Attended webinars hosted by Girl Up HQ.

COMMUNITY SERVICE AND VOLUNTEER WORK:

EMPLOYMENT EXPERIENCE:

_____

_____

_____

_____

_____

_____

_____

_____

_____

_____

SCHOOL-BASED EXTRACURRICULAR ACTIVITIES:

_____

_____

_____

_____

_____

_____

_____

_____

_____

_____

_____

LEADERSHIP ROLES, HONORS, AND AWARDS:

_____
_____
_____
_____
_____
_____
_____
_____
_____
_____

SPECIAL TALENTS OR HOBBIES:

_____
_____
_____
_____
_____
_____
_____
_____

Now go back and put a star next to the **five activities** that are most significant to you or speak directly to your interests. Keep those in mind not just when writing your résumé but also when you're thinking about which schools to apply to.

"No one is going to actually send out the application for you, but it's useful to get some family members around so you can say, 'Can you remind me of what makes me *me*?' It sounds like such a simple question, but it's the hardest to answer."

—Yara Shahidi

Keeping up with your classes, extracurriculars, and friends while also studying for the SATs, narrowing down college options, and figuring out financial aid can be . . . a lot. Like, *a lot* a lot. Are you experiencing stress, confusion, frustration, even burnout? **Sometimes writing about your challenges and stresses can make them more manageable.**

PUT YOUR THOUGHTS ON PAPER HERE:

_____

_____

_____

_____

_____

_____

_____

"The best thing to do is to be the most prepared you can be—if you do that, then you've done your job. You can say, I've done everything I can to make this as good as it can be. And then you just have to leave it up to the universe."

—Lea Michele

_____

_____

_____

_____

_____

_____

_____

College Options

There are many great schools out there to choose from. So how do you decide which ones to apply to? Use these categories to narrow down your choices.

	Pros	**Cons**
Private vs. Public	Class sizes tend to be smaller. More affordable.	More expensive. Usually has a larger faculty-to-student ratio.
Far Away vs. Close to Home	Opportunity to experience new things, meet new and different kinds of people, gain more independence. Opting out of dorm life saves money, and family and old friends are nearby to lend support.	Potential for homesickness; traveling during school holiday times can be expensive. Mom or Dad are always around, and it will feel like less of an adventure.
Big vs. Small	Lots of majors to choose from (you can switch from philosophy to physics) and lots of people to meet. A tight-knit vibe, familiar faces on campus, more chances to stand out.	You could feel invisible in a 400-person lecture hall, and you'll have to work harder to be on a first-name basis with your professors. Fewer things to do and not as many class offerings.

42

Pros

A strong school spirit and picturesque campus.

Lots of noncollege things to do and plenty of access to public transportation.

○○○○○○○○○○○○○○○○○○○○○○

Offers a more traditional experience and opportunities to meet boys (for friendship or romance, you decide!).

Every student leader is a woman, and you'll leave school with a super-strong network of alums.

Cons

You might blow your budget on gas just to find a decent burrito—or to get to the closest airport or train station for visits home.

Lack of common space, high cost of living, city noise 24-7.

○○○○○○○○○○○○○○○○○○○○○○

Potential for bro culture or old boys' clubs, like guys throwing shade in computer science class. (Not that you'd let that stop you!)

Potential for less diversity and less of a real-world feel.

Rural vs. City

Coed vs. Women's Only

Campus Culture

	Pros	Cons
Academic	No shortage of philosophical convos to engage in.	If you struggled through your AP courses, this setting may prove more stressful than satisfying.
Artsy	You'll be able to flex your creative muscles and find some people who appreciate poetry as much as you do.	If flashbacks of the school play give you hives, then . . .
Sports-Minded	You'll be able to play the sport you love, or spend Saturdays cheering on the home team.	If PE was your least favorite subject, or you have zero interest in learning the school fight song, you may get tired of trying to rouse those rah-rah-rahs.
Greek	You can find a like-minded squad, and you won't have to worry about filling up your social calendar.	If you're someone who needs dedicated alone time, or if you're just not interested in pledging, you might feel left out.

LIFE HACK: CHECK YOUR CHOICE

There are more than 4,000 colleges and universities across the country, which means there are *plennnty* of places to have an amazing experience. Instead of freaking out about finding The One, use this info to help focus your search—and weed out the options that are a definite waste of your time.

WHAT'S IMPORTANT . . .

A SOLID ROSTER OF MAJORS

Research shows that undergraduates switch their areas of study two to three times, so even though you may want to focus on art history now, make sure some of your other interests are offered too.

PROFESSORS YOU'RE EXCITED ABOUT

You shouldn't just look at available classes, but also who's teaching them, since one of your profs may become your mentor. It's a real bonus when you have teachers who have done something notable in your academic field.

[INSERT YOUR MUST-HAVE ITEMS HERE]

Come up with a few nonacademic things that would sweeten your experience—maybe it's good vegan food on campus or an active LGBTQ student body—and don't apply anywhere that doesn't meet those standards. With so many options, you don't have to settle.

AND WHAT'S NOT

YOUR PARENTS ARE ALUMS

There can be a lot of pressure to go to a legacy school. If you love where your mom or dad went, great! But if you don't, speak up. What worked for them may not work for you.

YOU'RE FOLLOWING SOMEONE THERE

Relationships change, and nothing is going to cause a case of "What am I doing here?" to set in faster than a breakup with your bae or BFF. Pick the college that's best for *you*. Maybe it's the same place as your bestie, but if not, just plan for lots of FaceTiming.

IT'S A "COOL" SCHOOL

Whether you're wowed by a big name that's ranked high on every list, a school with a championship sports team, or a celeb on campus, making your selection based on what's trendy could cause you to overlook what *wouldn't* make it a good fit.

what's best for ME??

When it comes to the next four years of your life, the non-academic part of school can be as important as the classes you take. Think about the social scene, the dining options, the nightlife, and the art and culture. **What are some things you must have, and some things you can do without?**

COLLEGE WISH LIST:

_____

_____

_____

_____

_____

_____

_____

_____

_____

_____

_____

_____

_____

_____

_____

_____

_____

_____

_____

YES!

COLLEGE DEAL BREAKERS:

_____

_____

_____

_____

_____

_____

_____

_____

_____

_____

_____

_____

_____

_____

_____

_____

_____

_____

_____

_____

> ## "Writing things down is such a brilliant way of getting things out and being so honest with yourself."
> —Ellie Goulding

Researching Where to Go

The more time you give yourself to find out about different colleges and narrow down your options, the easier the process will be come application time. Spend some time gathering info, then write down **five schools** that caught your eye.

1

WHAT DO YOU LIKE ABOUT THIS ONE? IS THERE ANYTHING ABOUT IT YOU DON'T LIKE?

2

WHAT DO YOU LIKE ABOUT THIS ONE? IS THERE ANYTHING ABOUT IT YOU DON'T LIKE?

3

WHAT DO YOU LIKE ABOUT THIS ONE? IS THERE ANYTHING ABOUT IT YOU DON'T LIKE?

_____

_____

_____

_____

_____

_____

_____

_____

_____

_____

_____

_____

_____

_____

_____

_____

_____

_____

_____

_____

_____

4

WHAT DO YOU LIKE ABOUT THIS ONE? IS THERE ANYTHING ABOUT IT YOU DON'T LIKE?

WHAT DO YOU LIKE ABOUT THIS ONE? IS THERE ANYTHING ABOUT IT YOU DON'T LIKE?

COOL

Ask a Student

You can learn a lot about a school from its website, but a better way to learn about what it's like day to day is to ask someone who actually goes there or recently graduated. Consider reaching out to connections, like a friend's older sister, or that guy from summer camp who enrolled last year. If you take campus tours, talk to the guides—they're usually current students, and it's their job to answer questions. (If you'd prefer privacy, ask if they'd be willing to chat when it's over.) Trust us, more often than not, people are happy to share their opinions.

Prepare yourself by coming up with a list of questions. For example:

- *What do you do on the weekend?*
- *Who wouldn't be a good fit at this school?*
- *How much time do you spend studying per week?*
- *What do you wish you'd known before starting?*

WRITE DOWN YOUR QUESTIONS HERE:

WHAT ELSE would you like to know about the school?

_____

_____

_____

_____

_____

_____

_____

_____

_____

"The only way you're gonna find out if you're in the right place is to stand in the place."

—Amy Poehler

_____

_____

_____

_____

_____

_____

_____

_____

Make the College Visit Count

You need to come away with a real sense of life on campus. Here's how to get the inside scoop:

Know before you go.

A college visit shouldn't be a blind date. Check out the school's Instagram and watch a virtual online tour first.

♥1

Wear something comfy yet polished.

You'll be walking a lot, so your #OOTD should be casual-chic— flats are fine; so are nice sneakers. If, however, you're meeting an admissions officer, wear the flats and skip that graphic tee.

Pick the right time to visit.

Go when classes are in session so that you can get a sense of the school. If you can, stay overnight so that you see campus after hours. This will give you a clue to the 24-7 life there. Don't forget to sign in at the admissions office. Some schools use it as a gauge of your interest.

what fitness options are available?

what are the dorms like?

Take a tour.

They're a great way to see the campus, ask questions, and observe the current students in their natural habitat. Make sure to plan ahead and register in advance.

Show yourself around.

Check out gathering spots, like the commons or the rec center, to pick up on the vibe. Know what you want to study? Ask an admissions officer or a prof in that department if you can sit in on a freshman class, visit the science lab, or swing by a rehearsal.

Read the student paper.

It'll help you learn what students care about. Grab a copy of the alumni mag, too, to see what programs the school values—and what successful grads are up to.

Ditch Mom and Dad.

Many tours have multiple guides who will eventually break up the group into smaller sections—bye, parents! Not only will you be able to ask what you really want (ahem, deets on the party scene), but you and your folks will have separate experiences to compare later.

Check out the town.

Be sure to swing by surrounding areas. Locate the important spots—the grocery store, the drugstore, the best pizza place—so that you'll know where to go if you want to spend time off-campus.

Do a recap.

Tours will blur together! Take pics during, then record yourself talking about pros and cons right after. It'll jog your memory when it's decision time.

**take notes & pictures

☆ ☆ ☆ ☆ ☆

SCHOOL: ....
_____

LIKED: _____

_____

_____

_____

_____

_____

_____

_____

_____

DISLIKED: _____

_____

_____

_____

_____

_____

_____

_____

_____

_____

_____

_____

THE RECAP

The more you can remember about your college tours, the better. Use the following space to take notes.

☆ ☆ ☆ ☆ ☆

SCHOOL: ....

LIKED: _____

_____

_____

_____

_____

_____

_____

_____

_____

_____

_____

DISLIKED: _____

_____

_____

_____

_____

_____

_____

_____

_____

_____

_____

_____

SCHOOL: ....

LIKED: _____

_____

_____

_____

_____

_____

_____

_____

_____

_____

DISLIKED: _____

_____

_____

_____

_____

_____

_____

_____

_____

_____

☆ ☆ ☆ ☆ ☆

SCHOOL: ....

LIKED: _____

_____

_____

_____

_____

_____

_____

_____

_____

DISLIKED: _____

_____

_____

_____

_____

_____

_____

_____

_____

☆ ☆ ☆ ☆ ☆

SCHOOL: ....

LIKED: _____

_____

_____

_____

_____

_____

_____

_____

_____

_____

_____

DISLIKED: _____

_____

_____

_____

_____

_____

_____

_____

_____

_____

_____

☆ ☆ ☆ ☆ ☆

SCHOOL: ....

LIKED: _____

_____

_____

_____

_____

_____

_____

_____

_____

DISLIKED: _____

_____

_____

_____

_____

_____

_____

_____

_____

FEELINGS AND STUFF: _____

It's typical to feel nervous when making a big decision, but if you get a sinking feeling at a particular school you visit, it may be a sign you aren't at the right place. To prevent jitters that may cloud your judgment, avoid excessive caffeine and get a good night's rest before your visit.

JUST WRITING: _____

What you do this vacay can help (or hurt!) your admissions chances.

Summer Plans a College Will ♥

check out volunteer opps

Keep your schedule manageable.

Think admissions officers will be impressed that you packed 25 activities into your summer? Uh-uh. Don't join things for the sake of joining—colleges like to see someone who focuses on activities they're actually interested in.

Do what you love.

Don't worry about your hobby or activity being too "out there." Admissions officers are open-minded, and they like students who will add something unique to the community.

Be committed.

A job at the grocery store might not seem impressive to you, but it can be to admissions officers. Whatever it is you're doing—whether it's bagging food or coaching young kids—be all in.

Try new things.

You may already have a major in mind, but don't obsess about matching your activities to that field of study. Do something out of the ordinary—it'll show your adventurousness.

Get some solid R&R.

Yes, we know you have stuff to do. But summer is the right time for downtime. Chill out, read a book, take a swim, hang with your besties—do whatever helps you relax. That way, you'll be refreshed and ready for your last year of high school!

senior

year

SENIOR YEAR

To-Do List

Fall

remember

[ ] **Ask for any additional teacher recommendations.** Remind the teachers you've already asked about your deadlines.

[ ] **Meet with your guidance counselor** to discuss which schools you should be applying to. While you're at it, ask about scholarships too.

[ ] **Take the ACT.** And, if you want to take the SAT or SAT Subject Tests one more time, register now.

[ ] **Check out the Common App** (www.commonapp.org) so you get a feel for it and see which schools require extra essays.

[ ] If you're applying "early action" or "early decision," **finish your essays** by the end of September.

[ ] During the first week of October, **submit transcript requests to your guidance counselor** for each school you're applying to.

[ ] **If you want to take the ACT one more time,** sign up for the December test. (Note: That will be the last chance to take it in time for application deadlines.)

[ ] **If you're applying "early action" or "early decision,"** complete your applications and submit them by the end of October.

[ ] **Check in on your transcripts and letters of recommendation** to make sure that they'll be in on time.

[ ] **Make sure your essay has been reviewed** by at least a few people before Thanksgiving.

REVIEWERS
1.
2.
3.

*Put all application deadlines in calendar!

Winter

[ ] **Complete your applications** before the end of December—be sure to check each school for its specific deadline.

[ ] **Submit any applications** at least 48 hours ahead of the deadline to avoid site outages due to submission overload.

[ ] If you have an early decision offer, **send in your acceptance.** (Congrats!)

[ ] As soon as your parents have their financial info available from the previous year, **start working on your FAFSA application** at fafsa.gov.

[ ] **Study for—and ace—your midterms!** Senior year grades matter to colleges, and some will revoke admission if your report card is a mess.

Spring

[ ] **Enjoy the end of your senior year** while you wait for those acceptance letters to start rolling in!

○○○

"When I was your age, I asked myself a lot of questions: what do I want to do? what am I good at? Is what I'm good at what I love? Or is it not? Now that I'm older, here's what I'd tell myself: FOCUS on what your HEART DESIRES and don't stop until you CAPTURE IT."

—Sarah Hyland

LIFE HACK: MEDITATION 101

One secret to slaying your stress? Meditation. You don't need to be an enlightened guru, and you don't need to go on a 10-day silent retreat. Anyone can do it, anywhere, at any time. All you have to do is breathe and take some time to focus on *you*.

FIND YOUR CHILL

1. Pick a place: Lie down at home, stand at your locker, sit down at your desk, or walk outside.
2. Inhale for a count of five, hold your breath for a count of five, then exhale for a count of five.
3. Repeat the breathing pattern for one minute, five minutes, or as long as you want!

WHAT'S YOUR MANTRA?

OM . . .

Having a word or phrase that inspires you or calms you (or both) is so helpful. Repeat it to yourself whenever you need a boost.

PEACE OF MIND

_____

_____

_____

_____

_____

_____

_____

_____

> # "Remember that a little discomfort isn't a feeling to shy away from—it means you're doing things right."
>
> —Melinda Gates, philanthropist

1 ....
....

This helps me: _____

_____

_____

_____

_____

_____

_____

_____

> Maybe you love to meditate, or maybe focusing on your breath is the very *last* thing you'd do to get mellow. So what are THREE THINGS you do to WIND DOWN?

2 ....

This helps me: _____

_____

_____

_____

_____

_____

3 ....

This helps me: _____

_____

_____

_____

_____

_____

_____

What is ONE NEW METHOD of getting calm that you want to try?

1 ....

....

How do you think this will help you? ___

_____

_____

_____

_____

Taking time to relax is as essential as brushing your teeth or washing your face. The more consistent you are about it, the more routine it becomes.

WHAT'S ON YOUR MIND? _____

Getting a Real Rec: Part 2

Give them time.

By early fall of your senior year, get the forms to the people you've asked for recommendations so that they have at least a month to write them. Some schools have a formal process for how to do this, so make sure you're following protocol. Check in a week before your recommendations are due to give people a friendly reminder.

Write an amazing thank-you note.

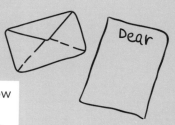

A handwritten note is a perfect way to show how much you appreciated someone's time and effort. Be specific about what the person did and how much it meant to you.

Set a deadline to send a thank-you.

Person writing recommendation:

_____

_____

For: _____

Due date: _____

_____

Person writing recommendation:

_____

_____

For: _____

Due date: _____

_____

Person writing recommendation: _____

_____

_____

For: _____

Due date: _____

_____

Person writing recommendation: _____

_____

_____

For: _____

Due date: _____

_____

_____

Before getting out the good stationery, PLAN what you're going to say first.

Dear _____

_____
_____
_____
_____
_____
_____
_____
_____
_____
_____
_____
_____
_____
_____
_____
_____
_____
_____
_____
_____

Sincerely, _____

Dear _____

_____

_____

_____

_____

_____

_____

_____

_____

_____

_____

_____

_____

_____

_____

_____

_____

_____

_____

_____

_____

Sincerely, _____

Essay Do's + Don'ts

In addition to seeing your grades and extracurriculars, colleges want to know how you think and write, and what you have to say. The application essay is your chance to speak your mind. Here are some general tips on how to do that well:

Do write about your interests! Even if you think your experience is pretty typical, your perspective isn't. So go ahead and brag about how perfecting your soccer kick sparked your love of physics.

 Don't simply rattle off a list of your accomplishments. Your achievements will appear elsewhere in your application. Use this space to discuss a different side of yourself or write about a meaningful experience you've had.

Do stay true to your experience. Be original and personal when expressing who you are and what's important to you.

 Don't write what you think the admissions officer wants to hear. Disingenuousness will come across on the page.

★ Not too formal, but not too casual

Do use words that you would really use in your everyday life. The real you is more refreshing.

 Don't use too many fancy SAT words. Trying to sound overly intellectual can actually hurt more than help you.

Do let your parents or someone you trust read your draft for spelling and grammatical errors. But . . .

 Don't let them do any deeper editing. An admissions officer can spot parental interference from miles away.

Before You Submit

Do take some time away from your essay. Revisit the draft later with a fresh brain—you might notice something you couldn't see before.

Do proofread, proofread, proofread! Make sure each essay is tailored for each college and that your grammar is on point.

Do read your paper out loud. You might find missing words or clunky syntax when you speak it.

Do print it before hitting submit. Online forms can be buggy, so if you copy and paste your essay into one, the formatting could look weird or the end of it could get chopped off.

Left your essay until the last minute? Here's how to write one in 10 (easy-ish) steps:

1. Turn off your phone and eliminate distractions.

2. Don't overthink it—just get everything out of your head and onto the page.

3. Ask yourself: What point am I trying to make, and have I made it? If not, revise.

4. Edit for structure and organization.

5. Show your draft to a friend to get feedback.

6. Edit based on input that you think makes sense.

7. Edit for the smaller stuff, like grammar and punctuation.

8. Take a break.

9. Give it a final read.

10. Submit.

" YOU
GOT
THIS "

Ready for some practice? Try out this personal statement prompt from Florida State University, which uses the application from the Coalition for Access, Affordability, and Success (www.coalitionforcollegeaccess.org):

"What is the hardest part of being a teenager now? What's the best part? What advice would you give a younger sibling or friend (assuming they would listen to you)?"

PRACTICE ESSAY #1

_____

_____

_____

_____

_____

_____

_____

"Do things you're afraid of. Trust
your gut. Own your weirdness. Learn
as much as you possibly can. Explore
enough to get passionate about
something and then start pursuing it."

—Jessica Alba

_____

_____

_____

_____

_____

_____

_____

_____

Ready for some more practice? Try out this personal statement prompt from Princeton University:

"Using a favorite quotation from an essay or book you have read in the last three years as a starting point, tell us about an event or experience that helped you define one of your values or changed how you approach the world. Please write the quotation, title, and author at the beginning of your essay."

PRACTICE ESSAY #2

CHEAT SHEET

College Costs

Follow this guide and stress less about paying tuition.

Know the price.

You wouldn't walk into a store and assume you'd pay the same for every outfit, and the same goes for colleges. Check out College Abacus (collegeabacus.org), a site that lets you compare the costs of schools.

Estimate your aid package.

Before you apply, you can get an idea of what each school will offer you. Some college websites have an Expected Family Contribution or Net Price calculator. (To easily find it, Google a school's name and "net price calculator.") Enter your family's info and let it crunch the numbers. Check out Frank (frankfafsa.com) to get a financial aid estimate too.

Pay attention to deadlines.

Even though you can fill out a federal student aid application (FAFSA) on a rolling basis, get yours in as soon as possible. Schools do run out of aid, so you don't want to miss out on money because you put it off until the last minute.

If you get an offer, study your aid letter.

Unfortunately, not every university clearly identifies what is a federal loan (you have to pay it back) and what is a grant (you don't have to pay it back). Can't figure it out? Call the financial aid office and ask questions.

Know the truth about loans.

If you need one, federal ones are better than private ones (like from a bank). They have lower interest rates and more flexible payment options. Whatever amount you borrow, you'll need to borrow it again for each year of college.

Search for scholarships.

You can earn money for all sorts of things! Check out finaid.org and scholarshipamerica.org for thousands of choices. Be wary of sites that will "do all the work" or charge you to file paperwork. That's code for *scam*.

$$$

College is an investment.

Along with your time and energy, you and your family will likely be spending a lot of money there too. Consider cost as a factor in your decision-making process—and tuition is just the start! Below are things you'll have to pay for while at school. Write down how much you estimate you'll spend per year:

- Tuition (before financial aid) _____
- Travel (how you will get to/from school) _____
- Local transportation (include gas and other car-related expenses if you have them) _____
- Housing/food (what does the school charge for room and board?) _____
- Books _____
- Dorm essentials _____
- Cell phone _____

- Entertainment and personal expenses _____

Ready for some more practice? Try out this personal statement prompt from UC Riverside:

"Think about an academic subject that inspires you. Describe how you have furthered this interest inside and/or outside of the classroom."

PRACTICE ESSAY #3

HIGH SCHOOL PROBLEMS: _____

_____

_____

_____

_____

_____

_____

_____

_____

_____

_____

_____

_____

_____

_____

_____

_____

_____

_____

_____

_____

_____

_____

WTF

CHEAT SHEET

Confessions of a Former Admissions Officer

Curious about what colleges really want to see before they stamp a big red "Admit!" onto an application? Well, since you asked . . .

Double-check the instructions!

They worry when you can't follow instructions.

If an application asks for two letters of recommendation and you send a stack as thick as the script for *Star Wars*, admissions officers won't read them. More important, sometimes when students send in 10, 15, or 70 (yes, it happens) letters, it seems like they're overcompensating for something. Pick the two best recommendations.

They want you to come prepared to your interview.

Do your research before you arrive, and come up with questions about things you truly care about. It's a win-win—you'll get the information you need to make an informed decision, and they get to know the real you.

They love when you show interest—but not too much.

Don't try too hard. Legend has it that a prospective student, when asked to share something surprising about herself, revealed that her nickname was Twinkie. Perfect. Then a week later, she sent a box of Twinkies to the admissions officer. Not so perfect. A handwritten thank-you note from Twinkie would have been enough.

Remember: They're not against you.

Want to know a surprising little secret? Admissions officers really want to love you.

"You don't need to wait to get to college to find your confidence. Take whatever it is you like about yourself—even if it's your pinkie toes—and walk around every day saying, 'You know what? I have really great pinkie toes.' Eventually that positive feeling will seep into every part of who you are, and the people around you will see it too."

—Uzo Aduba

Ready for some more practice? Try out this personal statement prompt from Colorado State University:

"The lessons we take from obstacles we encounter can be fundamental to later success. Recount a time when you faced a challenge, setback, or failure. How did it affect you, and what did you learn from the experience?"

PRACTICE ESSAY #4

Decision Time

Congratulations, you've been accepted! All of that SAT prep and time spent on the Common App totally paid off. But now that your letters are open, you may be feeling unsure about what to do next. Deep breath. This is how to handle it.

Accept (obviously!), but not right away.

Remember: Letters trickle in at different points, so you don't have to jump on the first offer you receive. There's time to think over your options before you decide. All schools require you to accept and submit your deposit (typically anywhere from $500 to $1,000) by May 1. Don't miss the deadline!

Have "The Talk" about cost.

This is when going to college gets real, and you need a solid plan for how you're going to pay. If you already filed your FAFSA, financial aid info will either be in your acceptance packet or arriving soon after. Make sure you understand the terms.

Tell the other schools.

If you got more than one acceptance letter (hello, boss babe!) and you feel confident about which ones you *don't* want to go to, let them know. That way, they can give your spot to someone else and redistribute your financial aid. Also known as: college karma.

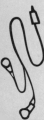

Take time to relax.

You don't have to do *all* the things right now. A few weeks after you accept a college offer, you should receive info about signing up for orientation, picking a dorm, and other fun stuff. If you don't get it by early summer, call the school's admissions office to follow up. But for now: Celebrate!

FAFSA fail?

Flaked on filling out your financial aid application? The good news: It's not too late. You can still apply. Just do it RN! You can also find more info on paying for college at fafsa.ed.gov.

LIFE HACK: REJECTION

Getting a "no" sucks, especially when it comes from a college you love. But you can overcome the blow and move on. Trust.

OWN THE FACT THAT YOU'RE UPSET . . .

Don't try to stop the feeling—to get better, you're going to have to deal with it. Start by outwardly expressing your emotions (maybe that's ripping up the rejection letter, or letting off steam with a sweat sesh). Admit to at least one person that you're disappointed, and then do something nice for yourself. (Starbucks date with your bestie?)

. . . THEN WAKE UP TO YOUR AWESOMENESS

The admissions committee has to make decisions in a somewhat arbitrary fashion, and they're not rendering a definitive verdict on your potential. So yeah, you didn't get in, but you're still badass AF.

PICK A NEW FAVORITE ☆ ☆ ☆ ☆ ☆

When it comes to schools, finding The One is a total myth. There are plenty of places where you can be happy. Hit up the websites of the schools that accepted you. This will help you get excited about what life could be like there. If you're close, visit the campus again. Seeing yourself there as an admitted student is different from touring as a prospective one.

LET IT GO

You've been living and breathing SATs, admissions interviews, and campus visits for what feels like forever now, so it's easy to forget that there's life outside the college bubble. Make your acceptance decision—and embrace it. And remember, nothing's set in stone. Give it a chance, and if you're not into it after a year, you can transfer to somewhere that might be a better fit.

WERE YOU WAIT-LISTED?

It can be frustrating—especially when everyone from your bestie to your bae knows where they're headed. Do this if you're in limbo:

Make plans to go elsewhere. Your dream college may still be a possibility, but you should send your deposit to another school in the meantime. And get excited about it.

Share any good news. Did your final semester grades skyrocket or did you win an award? E-mail admissions with anything new and impressive. It shows you're still excited about attending.

How do you cope with conflict, failure & rejection?

QUIZ

1. You flunked a big test. How do you deal?

a. You learned your lesson for next time.

b. Ugh, but whatever.

c. Drop the class. The teacher has it out for you.

2. The weather is screwing with your spring break plans, so you . . .

a. Go to plan B: weekend movie marathon, FTW!

b. Get bummed that you spent money on a new swimsuit, but at least you'll be ready for summer.

c. Feel frustrated AF. Nothing ever goes right for you.

3. If you're feeling annoyed, you . . .

a. Turn to your Headspace app.

b. Deal with it on the fly.

c. Pop off!

YOUR SCORE

Mostly As: Your positive attitude gives you a good mood advantage.

Mostly Bs (or a mix of letters): You try to have an upbeat outlook, but there can be drama.

Mostly Cs: You have one mode when you're stressed: agitated. (Go back to page 80 for tips on meditating.)

HOW DO YOU FEEL ABOUT _____
GRADUATING HIGH SCHOOL? _____

_____

_____

_____

_____

_____

_____

_____

_____

_____

_____

_____

_____

_____

_____

_____

_____

_____

_____

TAKE A MOMENT TO THINK BACK ON YOUR HIGH SCHOOL EXPERIENCE.

If there was one thing you could DO OVER, what would it be?

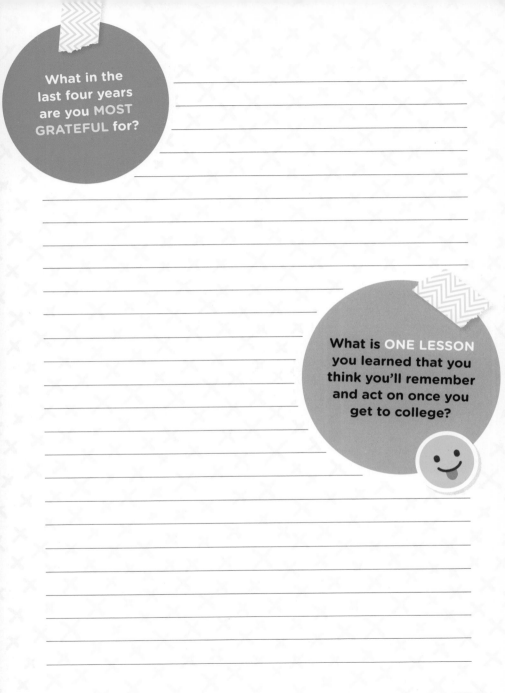

What in the last four years are you MOST GRATEFUL for?

What is ONE LESSON you learned that you think you'll remember and act on once you get to college?

127

before you go

[ ] If you haven't already, **follow your school on social media** so you'll be up-to-date on everything happening on campus.

[ ] **Study your college's course catalog.** Understand the required credits and classes you have to complete in order to graduate on time. Remember: Don't overload yourself with a super-tough schedule first semester. You may need time to get used to college-level work.

[ ] **Take care of yourself.** Eat well, get plenty of sleep, make sure you move your body. Reminder: All of these things affect your physical and mental health.

[ ] **Buy what you need for dorm living:** a shower caddy and flip-flops, mini reading light, extra-long twin sheets (look for ones with pockets), bed risers (with outlets), laundry bag, space-saving hangers, a mini fridge.

[ ] **Have fun with your friends**—and plan how you will stay in touch.

[ ] **Look up off-campus spots** in your college town so you'll know where to grab a bite, watch a movie, or take a walk.

[ ] **Be nice to your parents.** They worked hard to get you where you are, too, and they're going to miss you.

[ ] **Remember to:**

[ ] Plan to:

GOALS for
Freshman Year

1.

2.

3.

"Try something that is hard. Maybe fail. Learn something in your failure, and accept that you can't be the best at everything. Identify your STRENGTHS and make the most of them. The smartest thing you can do is push yourself to find challenges."

—Ellie Kemper

Future class of '

LIFE HACK: FREEDOM 101

Congratulations! You've graduated from high school. You're about to start a new phase of your life and step into the unknown. Uncertainty can inspire all kinds of feelings, from excitement to terror, anticipation to reluctance. Here are a few things to keep in mind.

BE OPEN

No matter how much research you've done, there's no way to know what college is really like until you get there. So check your assumptions before you arrive, and go in with an open mind—and an open heart.

YOU'RE NOT BEING GRADED

Okay, well, technically you are. But academic performance is only one part of your life. You've earned the right to more freedom, so explore your passions, the world, and your sense of self, without worrying about success or failure.

LOOK BEYOND YOURSELF

Self-consciousness has its perks; for example, it reminds you to inspect your teeth after finishing that kale salad. But if you get too caught up in your appearance or on how others perceive you, you'll miss out on what's happening around you.

EMBRACE UNCERTAINTY

There's no way to know what the world is going to throw at you. Like, ever. So just go with it.

_____

_____

_____

_____

_____

_____

_____

_____

_____

_____

_____

_____

_____

"The one thing you can control is what you bring to the room—or your college or the world. Prepare as much as you can, and have faith that your abilities will shine through. As long as you do that, you've done your job; everything else is out of your hands."

—Phillipa Soo

#HUSTLE

#WERK

Pause and take a breath. VISUALIZE what your *first day* on campus is going to be like. How you feel, how you meet people, what you do to get oriented.

Adulting 101

Hello

Make a killer first impression.

Your initial interaction with someone really does matter. Research shows we judge people within one-tenth of a second of meeting them. To make an immediate connection, look a person in the eye, and then give a firm handshake—it conveys a sense of confidence and trustworthiness. Keep the good vibes going by maintaining eye contact while you're chatting, and mention the person's name when saying goodbye—it shows you were truly engaged.

Own an awkward moment.

The secret to rising above a super-embarrassing moment? Use humor to call yourself out! For example, if you trip in front of a crowd, say, "OMG! Please tell me someone filmed that! I want to post it!" TBH, whatever happens, it likely isn't as big a deal as you think—most people are probably too wrapped up in Snapchat to notice your blunder.

#THESTRUGGLEISREAL

IMAGINE WHAT THE NEXT *YEAR* OF YOUR LIFE IS GOING TO BE LIKE.

What are you most AFRAID of?

What are you most **EXCITED** about?

What **ASSUMPTIONS** do you have?

QUIZ

How self-assured are you?

1. Does social media stress you out?

a. No way! Selfies are fun!

b. Sometimes. Why do people gotta be so rude?

c. You dream of the day you can delete all of your accounts.

2. A friend made a weird comment about you. How do you feel?

a. Not even sweating it.

b. It was ruling your thoughts—but then your crush walked by.

c. Anxious. Now you're analyzing every text she has ever sent.

3. Have you ever changed who you are to make other people happy?

a. And make *myself* unhappy? Never.

b. Yes, but I regretted it.

c. I need people to like me no matter what.

YOUR SCORE

Mostly As: You're the queen of brushing off haters, which keeps you in a Zen state of mind.

Mostly Bs (or a mix of letters): Your status: steady—most of the time.

Mostly Cs: You worry too much about what others think.

LIFE HACK:

KEEP OLD FRIENDS

Getting ready to spend time apart from your squad?
Make the distance NBD by staying connected.

GO BIG BEFORE YOU GO   #SQUADGOALS

Make your last days together an event. Host a theme party,
throw an old-school sleepover, plan a camping trip. Pack in
fun times that will become great memories.

MAKE A FUTURE FRIEND TRADITION

Figure out when you and your crew will be back in town, and get
something on the calendar—for example, brunch the morning
after Thanksgiving or a barbecue on the Fourth of July.

FORGET FOMO

Much of the anxiety that comes from separation is about
the fear of being replaced or forgotten. Keep your besties in the
loop by sending them pics of your new life—your dorm room,
your favorite off-campus hangout, or selfies from the quad.

SCHEDULE TIME TO CHAT

Continuing your Snapchat streak is cool, but calling or
FaceTiming for a real-time conversation can give you a
chance to go deeper and keep the connection feeling fresh.

PICK AN SOS EMOJI

Sometimes you might just need your bestie. Choose an emoji that will signal that you need to talk, *like*, now. Consider it your squad's secret code.

MAKE NEW FRIENDS

JOIN IN

It's hard to make friends alone in your dorm room. Go out and do something—join a club sport, try out for the a capella group, get a job. That's the best way to meet people who share your interests.

BREAK THE ICE

Sounds simple, but if you're shy, making that first contact can be a stretch. Do it anyway. Smile at someone, say hi, or give a fellow frosh a genuine compliment. Who knows? You might just meet your BFF.

BE REAL

Don't try to act like someone else. You're fine just the way you are. Forget the facade and just be yourself.

THINK ABOUT YOUR CURRENT FRIENDS.

HOW did you make the friends you have now?

WHAT is it you like about your current friends?

What MAKES a great friend?

You know the things you like about your current friends? Look for those same qualities in the new people you meet.

#BFF

THINK ABOUT MAKING NEW FRIENDS.

What EMOTIONS come up? Are you nervous? Excited? Write down any thoughts or feelings you have about making friends.

Sex, Drugs, and Decisions

Whatever your past experience is with drinking, drugs, and hooking up, you'll likely be facing new freedoms and new choices at college. And the decisions you make could have significant consequences.

Slow down.

The area of your brain that controls heat-of-the-moment impulses is the last part to mature—that happens in your 20s. So while you're still capable of making smart decisions, it's worth pausing so your brain has time to weigh in.

Your body, your future.

There's a lot in the world that you can't control. At the same time, you have the power to take care of your body and your life. So think about your goals and make choices that align with them. The most important thing: Stay safe!

Build trust.

There's no way to know everything about a situation or a person before you get involved. But establishing some kind of buddy system is essential for your safety—for example, when going out to a party, make a pact with a friend to keep an eye out for each other. And if you're thinking about hooking up with someone you don't know all that well, ask yourself: Do you trust this person to respect you and what you communicate? Do you trust yourself to speak up and stick to your boundaries? If the answers to these questions are no, your next move is worth reassessing.

Voice your choice.

If you want to be the master of your own life, you have to know your desires and boundaries and be able to clearly communicate them. Ask yourself: How do you feel about drinking and drugs? How do you feel about sex? In what ways might you be vulnerable to peer pressure?

If someone you don't know offers to refill your drink, say no. Anyone who dares you to drink more or tries to pull you away from your friends is bad news. And you should never, ever be intimidated, coerced, or forced to do anything you don't want to do—especially when it comes to hooking up or having sex.

Remember, consent is key: Yes means yes and no means no. Full stop.

If you want to learn more about sexual assault—or need help— visit the Rape, Abuse, and Incest National Network at <u>rainn.org</u>.

153

COLLEGE BUCKET LIST:

{free}

Adulting 101

Help a drunk friend.

Rule #1: No matter how much she's had, Do. Not. Let. Her. Drive. Also, you may have heard that giving someone coffee or getting them some fresh air will sober them up. Unfortunately, none of those things actually work. **Instead, here's what you should do:**

If she's not acting like herself.

You may be getting annoyed she's belting out "Sorry" by the Biebs for the hundredth time, but stay chill. People who have been drinking can get agitated fast, and you don't want the situation to spiral out of control. Don't let her drink any more.

If she's stumbling and slurring.

It's time for you both to exit—she needs to sleep it off. Suggest that she stay at your place, so you can keep an eye on her. (Promise to bring her breakfast in bed as an incentive.) If she's vomiting, make sure she stays awake and is coherent.

If she's passed out.

If she's barely with it or not responsive, you need to call 911. Her life is far more important than any other consequences. While you wait for help, don't try to give her food or water. It could cause her to choke if she has alcohol poisoning.

_____

_____

_____

_____

_____

"College really does help you grow up and figure out who you are. So, it's just helped me grow as a person, like even just getting to classes on time and figuring out where classes are."

—Miranda Cosgrove

_____

_____

_____

_____

_____

_____

_____

_____

_____

See Ya, Stress

It's normal to feel stressed sometimes, and there's pretty much a guarantee it'll happen at college. It's very important that you have ways to cope when you feel overwhelmed. **Here are some ways to deal, and some to steer clear of.**

Talk it out.

FaceTime your BFF from back home; dial up your parents; or vent to your new group of friends. It'll feel comforting to talk to the people who know you well— or people who can relate to what you're going through.

Get wasted.

Drinking or taking drugs might make you forget for a minute, but they actually make you feel worse in the long run. And remember, they can be dangerous and addictive too.

Laugh.

Watch dog clips on YouTube, whatever makes you crack up. Laughing helps your body release stress.

Eat well.

Junk food—think high-sugar (candy bars, cookies), super-processed carbs (Flamin' Hot Cheetos. . .), and high-fat (burgers and fries)—drags down your energy and mood. But it can be hard to keep up healthy habits in your new routine. To feel your best, aim to eat regular, balanced meals and fill up on lean protein (chicken, tofu), fruits and veggies, beans, healthy fats (avocado), and complex carbs (brown rice, wheat bread).

Guzzle another coffee.

Getting wired—especially when you sip in the afternoon or later—disturbs your sleep, which can make stress, focus, and concentration worse.

Exercise.

Run a mile around the track or catch a yoga class—or do any heart-pumping activity you've always loved. Exercise can decrease stress hormones and boost happy endorphins.

Pull an all-nighter.

Go to bed at a decent hour, especially if you're studying for a test. Sleep helps your brain store information and memories—so snoozing will help your grades.

Studies show that listening to music or watching underwater creatures swim (seriously!) can help BOOST YOUR MOOD. What makes you feel better when you're down?

1 ....

....

This helps me: _____

_____

_____

_____

_____

_____

_____

_____

_____

_____

2 ....

This helps me: _____

_____

_____

_____

_____

_____

_____

_____

_____

_____

_____

3 ....

This helps me: _____

_____

_____

_____

_____

_____

_____

_____

_____

_____

1 ....
....

How do you think this will help you?

_____

_____

_____

_____

_____

_____

_____

What is one new COPING METHOD that you want to try?

If you're struggling with anxiety or depression and need help, visit your campus counseling center. Need immediate help? The Crisis Text Line has counselors available 24-7; just send a text to 741-741. Or call the National Suicide Prevention Lifeline at 1-800-273-TALK. In an emergency situation? Dial 911.

Adulting 101

Be a pro at laundry.

The basic plan: Sort it by color (mix darks and whites and you'll end up with tinted underwear!) and also by fabric (keep delicates away from denim). Make sure to read all the instructions, from the detergent bottle (using too much can trap dirt in your stuff) to the tags on your clothes (some items need to be washed on a certain cycle). A hack to wash away your rookie status: Pull everything out of the dryer 10 minutes before it's done and you won't have to iron!

How to fight stains:

Ink	Rub with rubbing alcohol, hand sanitizer, or hair spray, then rinse with cold water.
Chocolate	Scrape off excess, then put a drop of clear dish soap on it.
Makeup	Rinse away any pigment without rubbing, then treat with a stain remover.
Food grease	Treat the area with stain remover.
Tomato	Apply stain remover, then dab on white vinegar and gently rub with a toothbrush.
Gum	Put the item in the freezer till the gum is hard, then peel it off.
Blood	Dab the area with hydrogen peroxide.

Make Money Work for You

Most college students aren't exactly rolling in dough. So be smart when it comes to the moolah you do have. Here's some common "cents" advice to help you take control of your cash flow.

Put it in the bank.

If you have a side hustle—even if it's just occasional petsitting—set up a checking account. Having one will help you be more aware of where your earnings are going. If you're managing your own money at college, you'll need a debit card and checks to pay bills and buy supplies.

Stash some away.

A good rule of thumb is to sock away 10 percent of your income. Set up a savings account, which is different from a checking account because it earns interest. (Free money!) If the rate seems low, don't sweat it—even a small amount helps your balance grow if it sits untouched.

Shop smarter.

The next time you're browsing at your fave store, remember this: Research shows that if you hold something for 30 seconds or longer, you're more likely to buy it. So avoid toting around every item you want.

DIY Life

College may be the first time you have to take care of yourself on a daily basis. Want clean clothes? It's up to you to do your laundry. Want to avoid debt? Pay off your credit card monthly. Want to get to class on time? Then go to bed at a reasonable hour and set your alarm.

What are some important ADULTING SKILLS you've yet to master? (If you can't think of any, ask a parent—they'll be more than happy to give you some ideas!)

NOW's the
time to start
practicing!

Are you a big spender or a penny-pincher?

To find out, mark the statements that sound like the ways you handle your cash flow, then use the key at right for the answer.

A

[ ] You're all about having fun and splurging.

[ ] You and your friends eat at nice restaurants several times a week.

[ ] If you found $20, you'd quickly use it to buy yourself a present.

[ ] When you hear about a party, you head to the mall for an entirely new outfit.

[ ] Your attitude: Shop now, worry later.

[ ] You know how much money you have in the bank—the ATM just said you had none available.

B

[ ] Mini gigs that pay (chores, babysitting) are your thing.

[ ] Chipotle is your squad's second home.

[ ] Found money? Great! That pays for a few lunches this week.

[ ] When there's a party on your calendar, you treat yourself to a mani.

[ ] You have your eye on an ultra-cool pair of sunnies, but you're holding out for a sale.

[ ] You check your bank balance every week or so.

C

[ ] You've scored a steady job.

[ ] Does a sandwich in the park count as a meal out?

[ ] Any unexpected cash goes straight into your college fund.

[ ] Your only party prep: getting your go-to dress out of your closet.

[ ] You see the perfect skirt but tell yourself that you don't need it.

[ ] You have a checking and a savings account (and always know how much is in them).

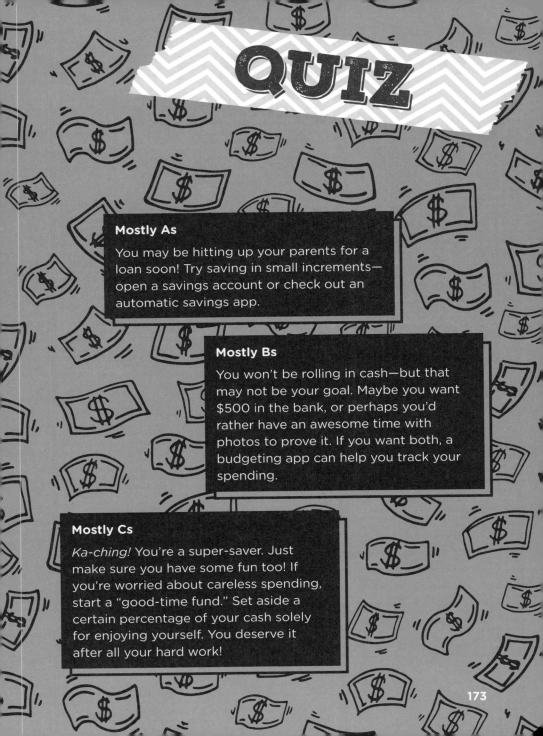

QUIZ

Mostly As

You may be hitting up your parents for a loan soon! Try saving in small increments—open a savings account or check out an automatic savings app.

Mostly Bs

You won't be rolling in cash—but that may not be your goal. Maybe you want $500 in the bank, or perhaps you'd rather have an awesome time with photos to prove it. If you want both, a budgeting app can help you track your spending.

Mostly Cs

Ka-ching! You're a super-saver. Just make sure you have some fun too! If you're worried about careless spending, start a "good-time fund." Set aside a certain percentage of your cash solely for enjoying yourself. You deserve it after all your hard work!

_____

_____

_____

_____

_____

_____

_____

_____

_____

_____

_____

_____

SAVE $$$

The real sign of being an adult is that you aren't always asking your parents for cash, so it's time to get your own stash. A good way is to find a side hustle—something that will take only a few hours of your time. Aside from the typical gigs, like babysitting or tutoring, you could search for ones where you work from home. Reach out to local businesses to see if you can run their social media. Another idea? Look for a part-time job at a place where you always spend—say, a cool boutique, your fave coffee shop—so you'll get discounts!

#SLAY

_____

_____

_____

_____

_____

_____

_____

> # "Know your talent, know your gift, and be proud of yourself."
>
> —Meghan Trainor

_____

_____

_____

_____

_____

_____

_____

_____

_____

_____

_____

Résumé Revamp

Now that you have high school and a whole extra year of experience under your belt, it's a good time to update your résumé. (Because it's easier to remember accomplishments soon after you've achieved them, do this regularly.) Then, when you need to apply for a job, an internship, or even graduate school (whoa!), it'll be ready to go.

COMMUNITY SERVICE AND VOLUNTEER WORK:

EMPLOYMENT EXPERIENCE:

_____
_____
_____
_____
_____
_____
_____
_____
_____

SCHOOL-BASED EXTRACURRICULAR ACTIVITIES:

_____
_____
_____
_____
_____
_____
_____
_____
_____

LEADERSHIP ROLES, HONORS, AND AWARDS:

SPECIAL TALENTS OR HOBBIES:

"At college, I realized I could be whoever I wanted to be."

—Kristen Bell

Take a moment to think about next year. What are some things you hope to ACCOMPLISH, LEARN, or EXPERIENCE during that time?

college resources

General Advice

NACAC // nacacnet.org/knowledge-center/
knowledge-center-search

TPR College Advice // princetonreview.com/college-advice

College Confidential // collegeconfidential.com

College Search Websites

American Association of Community Colleges // aacc.nche.edu

eCampus Tours // ecampustours.com

The Women's College Coalition // womenscolleges.org

Smart Class // colleges.startclass.com

Big Future // bigfuture.collegeboard.org/college-search

College Data // collegedata.com

Niche // niche.com

Unigo // unigo.com

College Xpress // collegexpress.com

College Search Apps

MyOptions // admitted.ly

The College Fair // kickwheel.com

College Hunch // collegehunch.com

College Counseling and Tutoring Websites

College Match // collegematchus.com

KnowHow2Go // knowhow2go.org

Sylvan Learning Centers // educate.com

College Counseling Associates // cca4college.com

Ivy Coach // ivycoach.com

University Tutor // universitytutor.com

Chegg Tutors // chegg.com/tutors

Buddy School // buddyschool.com

E-Tutor // e-tutor.com

Wyzant // wyzant.com

Princeton Review // princetonreview.com/academic-tutoring

Standardized Test Help

ACT/PLAN // act.org

Education Testing Services (ETS) // ets.org

FairTest: The National Center for Fair and Open Testing //
    fairtest.org

SAT/PSAT/AP // collegeboard.com

Kaplan // kaplan.com

4Tests // 4tests.com

March2Success // march2success.com

Test Prep Review // testprepreview.com

McGraw Hill Practice // mhpracticeplus.com/act.php

Edupath // edupath.com or download the app

Financial Aid and Scholarships

CollegeNET // collegenet.com

College Scholarships Service (CSS) //
   profileonline.collegeboard.com

The Education Resources Institute—TERI College Access // teri.org

EduPASS // edupass.org/finaid

Expected Family Contribution Calculator // bigfuture.collegeboard
   .org/pay-for-college/paying-your-share/expected-family
   -contribution-calculator

FastWeb! // fastweb.com

FinAid: // finaid.com

Frank // frankfafsa.com

Scholarship America // scholarshipamerica.com

The Scholarship Coach // scholarshipcoaches.com

United Negro College Fund // uncf.com

FAFSA // fafsa.ed.gov

Princeton Review // princetonreview.com/college-advice/pay

RaiseMe // raise.me

My Scholly // myscholly.com

Scholarships.com // scholarships.com

Scholarship Monkey // scholarshipmonkey.com

SallieMae // salliemae.com

Seeds of Fortune // seedsoffortune.org

Student Scholarships // www.studentscholarships.org

College Scholarships // collegescholarships.com

Cappex // cappex.com

Petersons // petersons.com

Weird Scholarships // weirdscholarships.net

LendEdu // lendedu.com

Applications/Planning Tools

The Coalition for Access, Affordability, and Success //
coalitionforcollegeaccess.org

The Common Application // commonapp.org

Campus Lifestyle

College Fashionista // collegefashionista.com

Dormify // dormify.com

Fresh U // freshu.io

Spoon University // spoonuniversity.com